Games

by Ellen A. Goodenow

Harcourt

Orlando   Austin   Chicago   New York   Toronto   London   San Diego

Visit *The Learning Site!*
www.harcourtschool.com

Long ago, children played many games.

Today, children play many of the same games.

2

Children played
tag.

Children played **ball**.

They played
with **tops**,
too.

Children played **jacks**.

They played **jump rope**.

Which games
from long ago do
you play today?

8

Think and Respond

① What are some games that children play?
② Why do you think children today play the same games that children played long ago?
③ What game do you like best?

Write a Sentence Draw a picture of your favorite game. Write a sentence to tell why you like this game so much. Ask an adult to help you find out if this game was played long ago.

Word Count: 42

Created by TIME For Kids to accompany
Harcourt Social Studies Programs

ISBN 0-15-333121-6

90000>

9 780153 331213

T2-FPG-136

"Clara was sliding down the yellow slide, when
she saw a big yellow lion coming toward the slide."

'Hey,' she said, 'lions don't belong at the park,
they belong at the . . . .

. . . . JUNGLE!'

"So, the friends called for help and the lion went back to the jungle."

"Anna was playing on the cross bars,
when she saw a pink pig playing and having fun."

'Hey,' she said, 'pigs don't belong at the park
they belong at the . . . .

"So, Anna brought the pig back to the farm."

"Nora was going around on the merry-go-round,
when she saw a red turtle on the ground."

'Hey,' she said, 'turtles don't belong at the park,
they belong at the. . . . . . .

. . . . POND!'

"So, she started to walk with the turtle to the pond."

"Abby was watching three green frogs,
hop, hop, hopping on the ground."

'Hey,' she said, 'frogs don't belong in the park,
they belong in the. . . . .

.... POND!'

"So, she caught up with Nora, and they both went to bring the turtle and the frogs back to the pond."

"Jace was running across the field, and
almost ran into a big brown bear."

'Hey,' he said, 'bears don't belong in the park,
they belong in the. . . . . .

"So, he walked the bear back to the forest."

"When Jace got back to the park, he saw his friends watching the blue birds land on the cross bars."

'Hey,' they said, 'birds don't belong on the cross bars, they belong in the . . . .

. . . . . .TREES!'

"So they all ran around, waving their arms and hands at the birds and they flew away and landed in the trees."

Just after that, I woke up and couldn't remember my *mèmeŕe* finishing her story. I do remember dreaming about:

Orange puppies, yellow lions, pink pigs, red turtles, green frogs, brown bears, blue birds and . . . .

. . . . playing with my friends!

"I hope that you have fun playing with your friends."

Happy ending!

Sweet dreams!

Rosemary Turgeon is a registered nurse; she resides in Brewer, Maine with her husband of thirty-one years. She has three grown children and six grandchildren. She taught children for more than twenty-five years in many areas of ministry: Sunday school, Jr. Church, Neighborhood Bible Time, and AWANA, (a non-denominational children's ministry program). Most recently, she volunteers as an elementary school librarian at her local Christian school.

Her oldest granddaughter, Faith, was born with Down syndrome. She has had two open heart surgeries and has many health issues. She is a "ray of sunshine," to all who meet her. Faith, absolutely loves it when her *mèmére* tells her her favorite story, using her very special blankie. We pray that you enjoy, *My Very Special Blankie* as much as we have.

All proceeds from the sale of this book will go into an account for Faith.

CPSIA information can be obtained at www.ICGtesting.com
Printed in the USA
BVOW11s2357240914

368256BV00003B/3/P